"We're in t'

DRAGS

Dedication

This book is dedicated to the many colleagues and friends I have made during my working life. I have been very fortunate to have experienced more than one career and have made several direction changes in pursuance of my career goals. I have travelled extensively and experienced the world, life and extremes of human nature and spirit as a result. This has allowed me to develop an extensive knowledge base and skill set and facilitated the opening of many, many doors of opportunity that might have otherwise remained closed to the average person, but thankfully not to me. My chosen path has taught me many lessons and some of the most powerful have been what could be described as the more adverse and painful variety. I use what I regard as a poignant analogy when talking to peers and up and coming leaders of the future as follows:

"The best bosses I have had the experience of working with are the worst, most ineffectual and incompetent bosses. Why? Because they teach you how not to act or lead." From these I have developed my own style of working and I sincerely hope that I have made a difference for the betterment of my colleagues and service users, for that has been my driver.

One of the most important influencers that anyone can have in a career path are your work peers, who hopefully become life long friends, confidants and mentors. I have been blessed with an abundance, many of whom remain friends to this day and to these individuals I offer my thanks and appreciation for making the journey worthwhile. Good bad or indifferent you have all made a difference, you have influenced and helped to make me what I am (it's your fault).

"We're in this together"

Forward

In our fast-paced and ever-changing world, the realm of work life has undergone incredible transformations. As individuals, we are constantly striving to strike a balance between our professional aspirations and personal fulfilment. It is within this dynamic environment that we find ourselves seeking guidance, motivation, and inspiration to navigate the challenges and opportunities that lie ahead.

Welcome to this collection of Inspirational Quotes about Work Life. Within these pages, you will discover a treasure trove of wisdom, original quotes and a small selection of quotes from renowned thinkers, leaders, and visionaries who have left an indelible mark on the world of work. Whether you are an ambitious entrepreneur, a dedicated employee, a creative freelancer, or someone exploring their passion, this book is tailored to uplift and empower you on your unique journey.

Work life is an ever-evolving journey of self-discovery and growth. It is a place where we encounter triumphs and tribulations, setbacks and breakthroughs. Yet, in the midst of it all, we are reminded of the profound impact that a single word or a concise phrase can have on our perspectives and actions. These inspirational quotes encapsulate powerful lessons, encouraging us to embrace challenges, persevere in the face of adversity, and embrace the beauty of continuous learning.

As we immerse ourselves in this collection, we will encounter quotes that resonate with our experiences, others that challenge our perspectives, and some that provide the spark to rekindle our passion for our chosen paths. Each quote is a testament to the indomitable human spirit, igniting the fires of resilience and determination within us.

Remember, the journey of work life is not merely about reaching a destination; it is about cherishing the process and finding purpose in every step we take. As you read these quotes, allow them to serve as beacons of hope, guiding you through the darkest of moments and illuminating the path to success and fulfilment.

I invite you to delve into this collection of Inspirational Quotes about Work Life with an open heart and an eager mind. Let these words become the whispers of encouragement in times of doubt and the source of strength when faced with uncertainty. May this book inspire you to embrace your potential, unleash your creativity, and make a positive impact in both your professional endeavours and the lives of those around you.

Embrace the wisdom that lies within these pages and let it shape your work life journey into a remarkable and fulfilling adventure.

Here's to a future filled with courage, passion, and boundless opportunities!

"We're in this together"

Index

"Stay calm and composed, for your peace of mind is more valuable than their negativity."

*

Sometimes, difficult people try to provoke reactions, but staying calm allows you to respond wisely.

"Focus on solutions, not problems, and turn challenges into opportunities."

*

When facing difficult co-workers, shifting your mindset to seek solutions fosters a constructive environment.

"Seek to understand before being understood; empathy bridges gaps."

*

Try to understand their perspective and emotions before attempting to express your own, as it promotes mutual understanding.

"Stand tall, be assertive, and set clear boundaries; respect follows strength."

*

Setting boundaries with difficult individuals shows that you value yourself and expect respectful treatment.

"Choose battles wisely; not every disagreement is worth engaging in."

*

Prioritising your energy helps you focus on essential matters and avoids unnecessary conflicts.

"A smile can be your armour against negativity; spread positivity instead."

*

Radiating positivity can help defuse tense situations and inspire others to do the same.

"Listen actively; sometimes, all they need is someone who truly hears them."

*

Listening attentively can defuse tensions and create a more collaborative atmosphere.

"Focus on personal growth, for every challenge shapes a stronger version of you."

*

Embrace challenges as opportunities for growth and self-improvement.

"Don't take their behaviour personally; their struggles might be unrelated to you."

*

Remember that their actions might stem from their own issues, not necessarily directed at you.

"Practice patience; some people take time to change, but your patience can inspire transformation."

*

Patience allows space for personal growth and can inspire positive change in others.

"Lead by example; kindness and respect can be contagious."

*

Modelling the behaviour, you desire in others encourages a positive work culture.

"Choose positivity over negativity, even in the face of adversity."

*

Your positive attitude can be a beacon of hope for others and can diffuse negativity.

"Don't let their opinions define you; stay true to your values and beliefs."

*

Upholding your principles in challenging situations demonstrates strength of character.

"Focus on the bigger picture; their actions are just a small part of your journey."

*

Keeping your perspective broad can help you navigate challenges with grace.

"Build a support network; together, you can overcome any obstacles."

*

Surrounding yourself with supportive colleagues can provide strength and encouragement.

"Success is not the key to happiness; happiness is the key to success. If you love what you do, you will succeed in your work." - Albert Schweitzer

*

Explanation: Finding joy and fulfilment in your work will not only make you more productive but also lead to long-term success and personal satisfaction.

"Embrace challenges as stepping stones to growth, for they unlock your potential and lead to remarkable achievements in your work life."

*

Instead of fearing challenges, view them as opportunities to learn and improve. Embracing challenges enables you to expand your skills and capabilities, leading to greater success and fulfilment in your work.

"Find your work-life harmony, where personal passions and professional pursuits blend harmoniously, enriching both aspects of your life."

*

Seek a balance between your personal interests and career goals. When you align your passions with your work, you'll experience increased motivation and a sense of purpose, enhancing both spheres of your life.

"Cultivate a culture of collaboration and support, where teamwork fosters innovation and shared success in your work life."

*

Encourage a collaborative environment at work, as it sparks creativity and allows individuals to achieve more collectively. Celebrating shared achievements strengthens team bonds and motivates everyone to perform at their best.

"Rise above mediocrity by setting ambitious goals and maintaining unwavering focus on your journey to greatness in your work life."

*

Dare to dream big and set ambitious goals. Stay focused on your objectives, even when faced with obstacles, as this dedication will drive you toward extraordinary achievements in your work life.

"Rise above mediocrity by setting ambitious goals and maintaining unwavering focus on your journey to greatness in your work life."

*

Dare to dream big and set ambitious goals. Stay focused on your objectives, even when faced with obstacles, as this dedication will drive you toward extraordinary achievements in your work life.

"Stay curious and embrace a growth mindset, for continuous learning is the key to unlocking limitless potential in your work life."

*

Maintain a thirst for knowledge and a willingness to learn. A growth mindset enables you to adapt, innovate, and stay relevant in an ever-changing work landscape.

"Lead with empathy and compassion, for nurturing the well-being of others enhances the harmony and productivity of your work life."

*

Display empathy and kindness towards colleagues and team members. A supportive and compassionate work environment fosters a sense of belonging and strengthens professional relationships, leading to greater productivity and job satisfaction.

"Efficiency is the currency of productivity, invest wisely by optimizing your time and resources in your work life."

*

Prioritize tasks, set clear goals, and use time efficiently to maximize productivity. This disciplined approach enables you to achieve more with the resources available, enhancing your work life efficiency.

"Celebrate the journey, not just the destination, for finding joy in the process enriches your work life with fulfilment."

*

While reaching goals is rewarding, finding joy in the journey itself adds meaning to your work. Celebrate every step of progress and appreciate the process of growth and development.

"Dare to innovate and embrace change, for embracing evolution is the gateway to breakthroughs in your work life."

*

Embrace change as an opportunity for innovation and improvement. An openness to new ideas and adaptation drives progress and keeps your work life dynamic and relevant.

"Forge your path fearlessly, for those who blaze their trail in their work life leave an indelible mark on the world."

*

Don't be afraid to take unconventional paths or explore new territories in your work life. Those who dare to be pioneers can create lasting impact and inspire others to follow their lead.

"Empower others to succeed, for nurturing talents and supporting growth strengthens the collective achievements in your work life."

*

Encourage and support the growth of others. When you empower colleagues and teammates to succeed, you contribute to a positive and thriving work environment.

"Success is liking yourself, liking what you do, and liking how you do it." - Maya Angelou

*

True success comes from a combination of self-acceptance, passion for your work, and the approach you take to accomplish your tasks.

"Appreciate the beauty of simplicity, for elegance in execution brings clarity and efficiency to your work life."

*

Embrace simplicity in your work processes and solutions. A focus on elegant and straightforward approaches enhances clarity and reduces unnecessary complexities.

"Harness the power of perseverance, for determination and resilience pave the way to conquering challenges in your work life."

*

Persistence and resilience are key to overcoming obstacles and achieving success. In the face of adversity, tenacity keeps you moving forward.

"Balance ambition with contentment, for finding peace in progress sustains your motivation in your work life."

*

While ambition is essential for growth, contentment with your achievements along the way allows you to appreciate the journey and stay motivated for the long term.

"Seek mentors and be one, for the exchange of wisdom and guidance elevates the collective wisdom in your work life."

*

Establish mentorship relationships and be open to learning from others. Sharing knowledge and experiences nurtures a culture of continuous learning and growth.

"Unlock your creativity, for the art of innovation adds colour and brilliance to your work life canvas."

*

Cultivate your creative thinking skills to bring fresh perspectives and innovative solutions to your work. Creativity enhances problem-solving and adds vibrancy to your work life.

"In the tapestry of your work life, weave a thread of gratitude, for appreciation magnifies the joy of achievement."

*

Express gratitude for the opportunities and successes in your work life. Gratitude fosters a positive mindset and deepens the sense of fulfilment in your accomplishments.

"Lead with integrity, for honesty and ethics form the bedrock of trust in your work life relationships."

*

Demonstrate integrity and ethical behaviour in all your professional interactions. Trust is essential for building strong connections and collaborations in your work life.

"Strive not to be a success, but rather to be of value." - Albert Einstein

*

Focus on contributing value to your work and the people around you, and success will naturally follow.

"Sow seeds of positivity, for a fertile ground of optimism nurtures a bountiful harvest in your work life."

*

Cultivate a positive attitude and encourage optimism among your colleagues. A positive work environment fosters productivity, creativity, and well-being.

"Embrace diversity and inclusion, for a tapestry of unique perspectives enriches the fabric of your work life."

*

Embrace diversity and value the different backgrounds, experiences, and perspectives of your colleagues. Inclusive work environments promote creativity, innovation, and a sense of belonging.

"Seek inspiration from within, for true motivation arises from aligning your purpose with your work life journey."

*

Connect with your inner motivations and purpose to find genuine inspiration. When your work aligns with your values and aspirations, you'll be more motivated to excel.

"Be a lifelong learner, for knowledge is the foundation of continuous growth in your work life."

*

Commit to continuous learning and professional development. Embracing learning opportunities enhances your skills and expertise, making you a more valuable asset in your work life.

"Cultivate resilience, for the ability to bounce back from setbacks strengthens the fabric of your work life journey."

*

Build resilience to handle challenges and setbacks with grace and determination. Resilience allows you to navigate tough times and emerge stronger and more capable.

"Create a legacy of impact, for leaving a positive imprint in your work life sphere empowers future generations."

*

Strive to make a positive impact in your work life and leave a legacy that inspires and empowers others to follow suit.

"Balance ambition with gratitude, for appreciating the present enriches the pursuit of future greatness in your work life."

*

Maintain a balance between ambitious goals and gratitude for your current achievements. Embracing gratitude brings contentment and enhances your drive for future success.

"Harness the power of collaboration, for united efforts amplify the potential of your work life endeavours."

*

Embrace collaboration as it magnifies the impact of individual contributions. Working together allows for diverse skills and perspectives, leading to more significant achievements.

"Adaptability is the key to thriving, for a flexible mindset conquers challenges and fosters growth in your work life."

*

Cultivate adaptability and embrace change as an opportunity for growth and increased productivity in the work place.

"Embrace challenges as opportunities for growth, and your positivity will shine through even the toughest workdays."

*

Positivity at work begins with a mindset that sees challenges as chances to learn and develop. By welcoming these moments with open arms, you'll find that your enthusiasm and positive energy will carry you through the ups and downs of your job.

"Gratitude for the small victories can create a ripple effect of positivity that transforms your entire work environment."

*

Acknowledging and celebrating even the smallest accomplishments can have a profound impact on your outlook. Practicing gratitude fosters a positive atmosphere, motivating not only yourself but also your colleagues to appreciate and encourage each other's efforts.

"Build a support network of colleagues who uplift and inspire you, and your workdays will become more joyful and fulfilling."

*

Surrounding yourself with supportive co-workers helps you stay positive and motivated. Together, you can uplift and encourage one another, making the workplace a nurturing environment for personal and professional growth.

"Find joy in the journey, not just the destination, and work will become a fulfilling adventure."

*

Focusing solely on end goals can lead to frustration and disappointment. By embracing the process and finding joy in the journey, you'll stay positive and driven throughout your workday, making every step worthwhile.

"Maintain a healthy work-life balance to recharge and bring your best self to the office each day."

*

A balanced life is essential for sustained positivity at work. Taking care of your well-being outside of the office enables you to return each day refreshed, energized, and ready to face challenges with a positive attitude.

"Choose a job you love, and you will never have to work a day in your life." - Confucius

*

Explanation: Finding work aligned with your passions will make it feel more like a fulfilling journey rather than a burden.

"Cultivate a growth mindset, and you'll transform obstacles into opportunities for personal development."

*

A growth mindset believes that abilities can be developed through dedication and hard work. Embracing this mindset helps you view challenges as stepping stones rather than barriers, fostering a positive attitude towards continuous improvement.

"Be kind to yourself when mistakes happen, for self-compassion is the cornerstone of resilience and positivity."

*

Mistakes are inevitable, but how you handle them matters. Practicing self-compassion allows you to bounce back from setbacks, learn from your experiences, and maintain a positive outlook.

"Celebrate the unique strengths and contributions of each team member, fostering an atmosphere of positivity and cooperation."

*

Acknowledging and appreciating the diverse strengths within your team fosters positivity and a collaborative spirit. By celebrating each other's contributions, you build a supportive work environment that thrives on synergy.

"Take short breaks to recharge your mind and body, fuelling your productivity and positivity throughout the day."

*

Taking regular breaks improves focus, productivity, and overall well-being. Use these moments to relax, meditate, or engage in activities that rejuvenate your spirit and help you maintain a positive outlook.

"Challenge negative thoughts with positive affirmations, creating a resilient and optimistic mindset."

*

Replace self-doubt and negativity with uplifting affirmations. By reprogramming your thoughts, you can maintain a positive attitude, even during challenging moments at work.

- "Share appreciation and positive feedback generously, fostering a culture of support and encouragement."

*

Expressing gratitude and providing positive feedback to colleagues creates a virtuous cycle of positivity. It boosts morale, fosters camaraderie, and enhances the overall work experience for everyone.

"Stay curious and open-minded, embracing new ideas that fuel your passion and enthusiasm for your work."

*

A curious and open mind leads to continuous learning and growth. Embracing new ideas and perspectives ignites passion and enthusiasm, keeping your positivity alive and thriving.

"Find joy in helping others succeed, creating a positive impact that ripples through the entire workplace."

*

Supporting and cheering on your colleagues' success brings fulfilment and joy. Your positive attitude towards their achievements contributes to a supportive workplace culture.

"Create a clutter-free workspace to enhance focus and promote a positive state of mind."

*

A clean and organized workspace reduces distractions and contributes to a positive mental state. It allows you to concentrate on tasks and approach them with a positive mindset.

"Set realistic goals and celebrate progress, building confidence and sustaining positivity in the long run."

*

Break down your goals into achievable milestones and celebrate each accomplishment. This approach fosters a sense of progress, which is essential for maintaining a positive attitude throughout your journey.

"Learn to say 'no' when necessary, maintaining a healthy work-life balance and protecting your positivity."

*

Boundaries are crucial for your well-being. Saying 'no' when needed ensures you don't overwhelm yourself and enables you to maintain a positive outlook.

"Start each day with a positive affirmation to set the tone for productivity and success."

*

Begin your day with a positive affirmation to set a constructive mindset. This simple practice can boost your confidence and resilience throughout the workday.

"Practice active listening and empathy, strengthening relationships and building a harmonious work environment."

*

Being a good listener and showing empathy fosters trust and rapport among colleagues. A positive work environment thrives on understanding and compassion.

"Seek opportunities for professional development, cultivating a sense of purpose and positivity in your career."

*

Continuously expanding your skills and knowledge keeps you engaged and motivated. Investing in your professional growth contributes to a sense of purpose and positivity in your work.

"You are never too old to set another goal or to dream a new dream." - C.S. Lewis

*

Explanation: Your age should never hold you back from setting ambitious goals and pursuing your dreams in your career.

"Practice mindfulness to stay present and focused, nurturing a positive and attentive mindset."

*

Mindfulness practices, such as meditation and deep breathing, promote clarity and emotional balance. Being present and focused enhances your ability to tackle challenges with a positive mindset.

"Offer a helping hand to colleagues in need, creating a supportive and positive workplace community."

*

Helping others builds camaraderie and a sense of unity. Offering assistance when your colleagues need it strengthens the bond within the team, fostering positivity and cooperation.

"Adopt a 'solution-focused' approach, turning obstacles into opportunities for creativity and growth."

*

Instead of dwelling on problems, focus on finding solutions. A solution-oriented mindset empowers you to tackle challenges positively, unlocking your creativity and resourcefulness.

"Practice random acts of kindness, spreading positivity and joy throughout the workplace."

*

Small acts of kindness can have a big impact. Simple gestures, like offering a kind word or lending a helping hand, create a positive ripple effect in the workplace.

"Learn from past successes and challenges, using them as steppingstones to a brighter future."

*

Reflecting on past experiences provides valuable insights for personal and professional growth. Embrace your successes and learn from your challenges, using them to propel yourself forward with a positive outlook.

"

"We're in this together"

Take ownership of your attitude, recognizing that positivity is a choice within your control."

*

Positivity is a conscious decision. By taking ownership of your attitude, you empower yourself to choose positivity in every situation, regardless of external factors.

"The secret of joy in work is contained in one word - excellence. To know how to do something well is to enjoy it." - Pearl S. Buck

*

Strive for excellence in your work, as the satisfaction of doing something well brings immense joy and fulfilment.

"Laugh often and find humour in challenging situations, alleviating stress and fostering a positive outlook."

*

Humour is a powerful antidote to stress. Finding lightness and laughter in tough moments can shift your perspective and maintain a positive attitude.

"We're in this together"

"Encourage creativity and innovation, fostering a dynamic and positive work environment."

*

A workplace that encourages creativity breeds positivity, as employees feel valued and empowered to contribute their unique perspectives.

"Practice deep breathing exercises to stay calm and composed during stressful moments."

*

Deep breathing helps reduce stress and anxiety. Incorporating this practice into your routine keeps you cantered and composed, enabling you to approach challenges with a positive mindset.

"We're in this together"

"Express gratitude for your team's efforts regularly."

*

Always show you feelings for a job done well, it means so much to them to be noticed, to be thanked and feel appreciated.

"Embrace challenges as steppingstones, not obstacles. They fuel your growth and lead you towards success."

*

Explanation: Embracing challenges helps you develop new skills and knowledge, which are essential for career advancement.

"Collaboration is the key that unlocks the door to innovation and productivity in the workplace."

*

Working together with colleagues fosters creativity and productivity, resulting in a more efficient and successful work environment.

"Continuous learning keeps your mind sharp and your career path upward bound."

*

Never stop learning, as ongoing self-improvement and skill development are critical for career progression.

"Embody resilience, for it will carry you through tough times and propel you towards triumph."

*

Resilience enables you to bounce back from setbacks and maintain focus on achieving your goals.

"Mentorship empowers both the mentor and mentee, creating a powerful cycle of growth."

*

Being a mentor or seeking mentorship allows for valuable knowledge sharing and guidance, benefiting all parties involved.

"Celebrate your achievements, no matter how small. They are the building blocks of greatness."

*

Recognizing and celebrating your accomplishments boosts motivation and encourages further progress.

"Courageously embrace change, for it opens doors to new opportunities and discoveries."

*

Being adaptable to change allows you to seize opportunities and advance in the ever-evolving workplace.

"Efficiency is the currency of productivity.
Spend it wisely."

*

Prioritizing efficiency in your work
processes maximizes productivity and time
management.

"The only person you are destined to become is the person you decide to be." - Ralph Waldo Emerson

*

Take charge of your destiny by actively shaping your career path and embracing the person you want to become.

"Create a positive work culture; it's the fertile soil for career growth to flourish."

*

A positive work environment fosters creativity, teamwork, and employee satisfaction, leading to individual career progression.

"Seek feedback as a compass guiding you towards improvement and excellence."

*

Embrace constructive feedback as a means to refine your skills and become a better professional.

"Network like a spider, spinning connections
that weave your path to success."

*

Building a strong professional network
opens doors to new opportunities and career
advancement.

"Stay hungry for knowledge, for it is the compass that guides you to greater heights."

*

The thirst for knowledge and continuous learning is vital for personal and professional growth.

"Be a team player, for teamwork makes the dream work."

*

Collaborating with colleagues fosters a supportive work environment and leads to collective success.

"Innovate with purpose, and you will leave an indelible mark on your industry."

*

Innovation that addresses real needs and challenges sets you apart and drives professional progress.

"Time management is the art of balancing tasks, priorities, and dreams."

*

Mastering time management helps you stay organized and focused on achieving your career goals.

"Embrace diversity, for it enriches your perspective and propels innovation."

*

Valuing diversity and inclusion in the workplace fosters creativity and enhances problem-solving capabilities.

"Invest in building strong relationships; they are the pillars of success in the workplace."

*

Nurturing professional relationships fosters a supportive network that aids career advancement.

"Embody integrity, for it's the cornerstone of a successful and respected career."

*

Upholding ethical principles and honesty earns trust and respect from peers and superiors.

"Be a lifelong learner; the classroom of life
has endless lessons to offer."

*

Continually seeking knowledge and learning
from experiences ensures constant personal
and professional growth.

"Confidence is the fuel that powers your journey to greatness.

*

Believing in yourself and your abilities boosts self-assurance, making you more likely to seize opportunities and progress in your career.

"Be a problem solver, and you'll be the go-to person for success."

*

Being resourceful and proactive in finding solutions makes you a valuable asset in the workplace.

"Build your resilience muscles, and setbacks will only make you stronger."

*

Developing resilience helps you handle challenges and setbacks with grace and determination.

"Adopt a growth mindset; it's the catalyst for perpetual achievement."

*

Embracing a growth mindset allows you to see challenges as opportunities for learning and development.

"Seek inspiration from within, for it holds
the power to propel you forward."

*

Harnessing your inner motivation and
passion drives your desire to succeed.

"Be a bridge builder, connecting ideas and people to forge progress."

*

Facilitating collaboration and communication between teams and individuals leads to collective growth.

"Believe in yourself and all that you are.
Know that there is something inside you that
is greater than any obstacle." - Christian D.
Larson

*

Self-belief is a powerful tool that can help
you overcome challenges and achieve your
full potential in your work.

"Aim high, but appreciate the journey, for success is a culmination of efforts."

*

Setting ambitious goals while acknowledging the incremental progress made along the way leads to sustainable success.

"Learn from failures, for they are the steppingstones to mastery."

*

Embracing failure as a learning opportunity helps you refine your skills and become more adept in your profession.

"Authenticity is your superpower; embrace it, and you'll shine brightly in your career."

*

Being true to yourself and authentic in your interactions fosters trust and respect from others.

"Stay curious; the pursuit of knowledge is the compass guiding your career voyage."

*

Cultivating curiosity opens doors to new ideas, skills, and opportunities for career growth.

"Seize opportunities, for they are the
catalysts of transformation."

*

Recognising and acting upon opportunities
propels you forward in your career journey.

"Lead by example, and others will follow your path of excellence."

*

Demonstrating leadership through actions and integrity inspires others to follow and fosters a culture of excellence.

"Be adaptable like water; flow with change,
shaping your course to success."

*

Being flexible and adaptable enables you to
navigate through shifts in the workplace and
seize new opportunities.

"Balance ambition with patience, for greatness is a journey, not a destination."

*

Having patience while working towards ambitious goals ensures you stay focused and resilient in your pursuit of success.

"Be a mentor; your legacy will live on through the success of others."

*

Sharing knowledge and mentoring others contributes to a positive work culture and creates a lasting impact.

"Own your mistakes, for they are steppingstones to growth and improvement."

*

Taking responsibility for mistakes fosters accountability and demonstrates a willingness to learn.

"Cultivate emotional intelligence, for it guides your interactions and decisions in the workplace."

*

Developing emotional intelligence helps you navigate workplace relationships and understand the emotions of others.

"Your work is your own personal signature.
Make it remarkable." - Anonymous

*

Approach your work with creativity and
dedication, leaving a lasting impression on
those who experience it.

"Embrace diversity of thought, for it fuels creativity and innovation."

*

Valuing different perspectives and ideas enriches problem-solving and drives innovation.

"Be proactive, for success favours those who create their opportunities."

*

Taking initiative and being proactive in your work leads to greater recognition and advancement.

"Practice gratitude, for it grounds you in humility and appreciation."

*

Cultivating gratitude fosters a positive mindset and enhances your overall well-being in the workplace.

"Be a lifelong networker, and your web of connections will propel your career forward."

*

Building and maintaining a diverse network opens doors to new opportunities and collaborations.

"

The difference between ordinary and extraordinary is that little extra." - Jimmy Johnson

*

Going the extra mile in your work can turn something ordinary into something extraordinary.

"In the busy workplace, success dances with those who stay in rhythm with their priorities."

*

To thrive in a hectic work environment, it's essential to align your tasks with your core priorities. By focusing on what truly matters, you can maintain a productive and balanced work schedule.

"Like a conductor, master the art of orchestrating your time to create a harmonious work-life symphony."

*

Just as a conductor coordinates musicians to create beautiful music, managing your time effectively enables you to achieve a balanced blend of work and personal life.

"We're in this together"

"In the whirlwind of tasks, take a moment to breathe and let clarity be your compass."

*

Amidst the chaos of a busy workday, pause and regain clarity about your goals and objectives. This will help you navigate through challenges with purpose and efficiency.

"A cluttered desk mirrors a cluttered mind;
clear the chaos to find your path."

*

Organising your workspace helps declutter
your thoughts and allows you to focus better
on the tasks at hand, leading to enhanced
productivity.

"We're in this together"

"

Embrace adaptability, for it is the key that unlocks the door to conquering change in the workplace."

*

A busy work schedule often brings unexpected changes. Embracing adaptability empowers you to navigate through these shifts and embrace new opportunities.

"The most fruitful growth happens when you step out of your comfort zone amidst a bustling work environment."

*

Embrace challenges and take calculated risks in your career. Growth occurs when you challenge yourself beyond the familiar.

"A well-rested mind dances through a sea of deadlines, for it knows the value of self-care."

*

Prioritize self-care and rest, as a rejuvenated mind can tackle challenges more efficiently, even in the face of tight deadlines.

"Time spent on nurturing relationships at work yields a garden of collaboration and mutual support."

*

Cultivate positive relationships with colleagues to foster a collaborative and supportive work environment, which can significantly impact productivity.

"Busy schedules can be tamed with a warrior's focus and a sage's tranquillity."

*

Combining intense focus with a calm demeanour allows you to navigate the busiest of schedules with grace and efficiency.

"In the middle of difficulty lies opportunity."
- Albert Einstein

*

When faced with challenges at work, look for the opportunities hidden within them to grow and improve.

"Celebrate progress, no matter how small, for it fuels the fire of motivation in the workplace."

*

Acknowledge and celebrate even the tiniest achievements to stay motivated and inspired amidst a demanding work schedule.

"A marathon of tasks requires the pacing of a
seasoned runner."

*

In a busy work environment, maintaining a
steady pace is crucial to prevent burnout and
ensure consistent progress.

"Like a painter, infuse each day with vibrant strokes of enthusiasm and passion for your work."

*

Approaching your work with passion and enthusiasm can turn mundane tasks into fulfilling experiences, even during the busiest days.

"Efficiency is the compass that guides you through the labyrinth of a packed work schedule."

*

Being efficient and organized helps you navigate the challenges of a busy work schedule with ease and precision.

"When the storm of deadlines rages, find solace in the eye of productivity."

*

Stay composed and cantered amidst a flurry of deadlines, allowing your productivity to be the calm amidst the chaos.

"The magic of time management lies in the balance between 'what needs to be done' and 'what can wait for tomorrow.'"

*

Knowing how to prioritize tasks and manage time effectively is the secret to conquering a busy work schedule.

"A busy schedule is a canvas for creativity;
let your ideas paint a masterpiece of
accomplishment."

*

Embrace the challenges of a busy workday
as an opportunity to showcase your
creativity and problem-solving skills.

"A unified team weathers any workload storm with strength and resilience."

*

Building a cohesive and supportive team enables everyone to handle the demands of a busy workplace with greater ease.

"The pursuit of excellence knows no pause button; it only dances with determination."

*

Strive for excellence in your work, knowing that relentless determination is the key to success, even during the busiest times.

"In the maze of tight schedules, creativity finds its way to flourish."

*

Creativity thrives when you face constraints. Embrace the challenge of limited time to unleash innovative solutions.

"Workplace productivity blooms when nurtured with a balanced blend of discipline and flexibility."

*

Balancing discipline with adaptability allows you to maintain productivity while adjusting to unexpected circumstances.

"Embrace the art of saying 'no' to the non-essential, for it liberates your time for the truly impactful."

*

Learning to say no to tasks or commitments that don't align with your priorities allows you to focus on what matters most.

"The only limit to our realization of tomorrow will be our doubts of today." - Franklin D. Roosevelt

*

Overcome self-doubt and believe in your abilities to reach new heights in your work.

"A successful workday begins with a well-organised to-do list and the courage to execute it."

*

Start each day with a clear plan and the determination to tackle your tasks head-on, ensuring a productive journey.

"Amidst the rush of deadlines, a moment of reflection births the spark of innovation."

*

Taking time to reflect and think deeply amidst a busy schedule can lead to ground-breaking ideas and solutions.

"The beauty of teamwork shines brightest during the darkest days of a hectic work schedule."

*

A cohesive team can uplift and support each other during the most demanding times, leading to collective success.

"The power of resilience transforms pressure into progress."

*

Cultivate resilience to face the challenges of a busy work schedule, turning pressure into an opportunity for growth.

"In the fast-paced workplace, knowledge is
the compass that steers you to greatness."

*

Continuous learning and knowledge
acquisition equip you with the tools to
navigate the complexities of a busy work
environment.

"A proactive mindset nurtures a garden of possibilities in the workplace."

*

Adopt a proactive approach, anticipating challenges and taking preventive measures to avoid potential roadblocks.

"In the midst of a hectic work schedule, be a beacon of positivity that lights up the path to success."

*

Your positive attitude can inspire and motivate others, fostering a constructive work environment, even during the busiest days.

"Adaptability is the sail that propels you through turbulent waters in the workplace."

*

Embrace change and adapt to evolving situations, as it enables you to navigate through the uncertainties of a busy work environment.

"Master the art of delegation to orchestrate a symphony of productivity."

*

Delegating tasks efficiently empowers you and your team to accomplish more, even in the face of a jam-packed schedule.

"Embrace the rhythm of continuous improvement, for it tunes the melody of excellence in your work."

*

Strive for constant improvement, as it allows you to refine your skills and deliver exceptional results.

"The strength of a united team transforms obstacles into stepping stones for progress."

*

A supportive and unified team can overcome challenges together, propelling each member toward success.

What you get by achieving your goals is not as important as what you become by achieving your goals." - Zig Ziglar

*

The journey towards your goals will transform you and help you grow, making the process as valuable as the outcome.

"Embrace the art of time-blocking to create a masterpiece of productivity."

*

Dividing your workday into focused blocks of time for specific tasks enables you to make steady progress without feeling overwhelmed.

'A busy work schedule is a testament to your value and contribution; embrace it with pride."

*

A demanding workload often reflects your significance and impact within the organization, so embrace it as a badge of honour.

"Courage is the wings that lift you above the clouds of uncertainty in the workplace."

*

Face challenges with courage and determination, knowing that your bravery will propel you beyond any uncertainty.

"Resilience is the anchor that keeps you steady in the storm of a bustling work environment."

*

Cultivating resilience allows you to weather any storm and maintain focus and composure during chaotic times.

"An organized mind orchestrates a symphony of accomplishments amidst a busy work schedule."

*

Organizing your thoughts and tasks contributes to heightened productivity, allowing you to achieve more in less time.

"The river of productivity flows when
fuelled by purpose and passion."

*

Identifying your purpose and aligning it with
your passion empowers you to work
efficiently and meaningfully.

"A well-crafted plan weaves the threads of success into the fabric of a busy work schedule."

*

A well-thought-out plan helps you make the most of your time and resources, enhancing productivity in the workplace.

"The art of work-life balance is a masterpiece of self-care and prioritization."

*

Balancing work and personal life requires thoughtful prioritization and taking care of yourself to avoid burnout.

"In the busiest of times, unity prevails as the ultimate strength in the workplace."

*

A unified team can overcome any challenge, drawing strength from collaboration and mutual support.

"Don't be pushed around by the fears in your mind. Be led by the dreams in your heart." - Roy T. Bennett

*

Allow your dreams and aspirations to guide you, rather than being controlled by fears or doubts.

"The tides of time wait for no one; ride the waves of productivity to success."

*

Time is a precious resource, and making the most of it through productivity leads to accomplishing your goals.

"A positive work environment is the fertile ground where success blooms."

*

Fostering a positive workplace culture cultivates productivity and enables individuals to reach their full potential.

"Embrace the ebb and flow of a busy schedule, for it unveils the rhythm of achievement."

*

Embrace the fluctuations of a busy schedule, as they reveal the patterns of productivity and accomplishment.

"In the pursuit of productivity, remember to pause and savour the sweet moments of success."

*

Celebrating achievements along the way boosts motivation and sustains your drive during a packed work schedule.

"As the conductor of your work-life symphony, choose to strike a harmonious chord of balance."

*

Taking charge of your work-life balance allows you to find harmony and fulfilment amidst a hectic schedule.

"The road to success is paved with focus, determination, and a willingness to adapt."

*

Stay focused on your goals, be determined in your pursuit, and adapt to the ever-changing landscape of work.

"In the fast lane of productivity, self-awareness steers you on the right course."

*

Understanding your strengths and weaknesses enables you to make informed decisions and optimize your performance.

"Like a puzzle, each task fits into the grand design of your success story."

*

Approach your work as a series of interconnected pieces that contribute to the larger picture of your achievements.

"The secret to mastering a busy work schedule lies not in doing more, but in doing what matters most."

*

Prioritization is the key to managing a busy schedule effectively. Focus on the most important tasks to achieve meaningful results.

'Success is not just about making money; it's about making a difference." - Unknown

*

Aim to create positive impacts through your work, and success will be more rewarding and meaningful.

"In the symphony of collaboration, every colleague plays a unique and essential note."

*

Each team member brings their own expertise and perspective to the table, making collaboration a powerful force in achieving shared goals.

"The dance of teamwork is an art, where trust and respect are the graceful steps that lead to success."

*

Trust and respect are the foundation of strong teamwork, enabling colleagues to work together harmoniously and accomplish great things.

"Supporting one another's growth is the nourishment that fuels the collective achievement of the team."

*

Encouraging the professional development of colleagues fosters a culture of continuous improvement, leading to overall success.

"Like stars in the night sky, every colleague
shines brightest when their individual
brilliance comes together as a constellation
of accomplishments."

*

When colleagues collaborate, their unique
talents and skills combine to create a
magnificent display of achievements.

"Success is liking yourself, liking what you do, and liking how you do it." - Maya Angelou

*

True success comes from a combination of self-acceptance, passion for your work, and the approach you take to accomplish your tasks.

"The power of teamwork lies not in being alike, but in respecting and embracing our differences."

*

Diversity within a team brings various perspectives and strengths, enriching the collaboration and enabling innovative solutions.

"A true colleague offers a helping hand without hesitation, knowing that their support elevates the entire team."

*

A supportive colleague willingly assists others, recognizing that collective success benefits everyone involved.

"A unified team weaves a safety net of encouragement, catching one another in times of challenge."

*

A cohesive team provides emotional support and encouragement, helping each other through difficult situations.

"The strength of a team blossoms in adversity, for it is in the face of challenges that true camaraderie is revealed."

*

Teams showcase their resilience and unity when confronted with obstacles, ultimately emerging stronger and more bonded.

"In the garden of collaboration, every seed of idea grows into a bountiful tree of achievement."

*

Nurturing ideas collectively leads to their growth and fruition, making teamwork a catalyst for success.

"An open mind is the bridge that connects colleagues' ideas, paving the way to innovation."

*

Welcoming diverse perspectives and ideas enables teams to explore new possibilities and push the boundaries of creativity.

"You are never too old to set another goal or to dream a new dream." - C.S. Lewis

*

Your age should never hold you back from setting ambitious goals and pursuing your dreams in your career.

"Embrace constructive feedback, for it is the compass that guides colleagues toward excellence."

*

Providing and receiving feedback with a growth mindset fosters continuous improvement and professional development.

"A sincere 'thank you' sows seeds of motivation, sprouting into a culture of appreciation among colleagues."

*

Expressing gratitude fosters a positive work environment, where colleagues feel valued and motivated to give their best.

"In the tapestry of teamwork, every thread contributes to the masterpiece of success."

*

Each colleague's contributions are integral to achieving the team's goals and creating a remarkable outcome.

"A united team celebrates not only victories but also the effort and dedication poured into the journey."

*

Recognising and celebrating collective achievements and efforts fosters a sense of pride and camaraderie within the team.

"The echo of collaboration reverberates with the melody of accomplishment."

*

Working together harmoniously results in outstanding achievements that resonate throughout the workplace.

'A supportive team serves as a trampoline of encouragement, propelling colleagues to new heights."

*

A team that encourages and uplifts its members inspires individuals to reach their full potential.

"The brightest ideas often emerge from the crossroads of diverse minds coming together."

*

Embracing diverse perspectives sparks creativity and innovation, leading to ground-breaking ideas.

"The strength of a team lies in finding common ground amidst diverse backgrounds."

*

Colleagues unite their differences to work towards shared objectives, leveraging their varied experiences for collective success.

"A strong team is like a puzzle; each piece complements the others to form a complete and cohesive picture."

*

Colleagues' contributions come together to create a unified and effective team, each piece being essential to the whole.

"In the realm of collaboration, generosity thrives as colleagues willingly share their knowledge and expertise."

*

Collaboration fosters a culture of sharing and learning from one another, propelling the entire team forward.

"Working alongside colleagues ignites the spark of inspiration that fuels the flame of motivation."

*

The energy of working together motivates individuals, leading to increased productivity and enthusiasm.

"In the garden of teamwork, positivity is the sunlight that nurtures growth and blossoms trust."

*

A positive attitude cultivates a supportive environment, fostering trust and camaraderie among colleagues.

"Choose a job you love, and you will never have to work a day in your life." - Confucius

*

Finding work aligned with your passions will make it feel more like a fulfilling journey rather than a burden.

"As colleagues, we are the architects of our own success, constructing a foundation of unity and determination."

*

Success is a collective effort, and colleagues build it through a strong sense of unity and a shared commitment to achieving goals.

"Colleagues are the sails that propel the ship of progress across uncharted waters."

*

Working together, colleagues steer the organization toward its objectives, even in uncertain times.

"The sum of our shared vision exceeds the value of individual dreams."

*

When colleagues align their visions and work towards a common goal, their impact multiplies, surpassing individual aspirations

"The symphony of collaboration becomes a masterpiece when each musician listens and harmonizes with the others."

*

Collaboration requires active listening and understanding, ensuring that colleagues work in harmony toward their shared objectives.

"In the embrace of teamwork, challenges become stepping stones to reach new heights together."

*

Teams thrive by tackling challenges collectively, using them as opportunities for growth and progress.

"A strong team is a shield of support, shielding colleagues from the storms of uncertainty."

*

In difficult times, a united team offers support and stability, making it easier for colleagues to navigate uncertainty.

"A shared sense of purpose binds colleagues together as they walk hand in hand towards a common destination."

*

A clear and shared purpose unites colleagues, driving them towards a collective vision of success.

"Doubt kills more dreams than failure ever will."

*

Embrace self-belief and let go of doubt to unleash your full potential in your career.

"In the tapestry of collaboration, we weave a legacy that extends beyond ourselves."

*

Through collaboration, colleagues leave a lasting impact, creating a legacy of shared accomplishments that live on.

"A flourishing team nurtures the seeds of empathy, compassion, and understanding, reaping a harvest of synergy and productivity."

*

A supportive team environment, characterized by empathy and compassion, fosters synergy and elevates productivity.

"Like a garden of different flowers, each colleague blooms with unique strengths that contribute to the team's vibrant ecosystem."

*

Embracing colleagues' individual strengths creates a diverse and dynamic team where everyone's contributions are valued.

"We're in this together"

"The strength of a team lies not in its absence of conflict, but in its ability to address and overcome challenges together."

*

A healthy team acknowledges and addresses conflicts constructively, strengthening relationships and finding resolutions.

"A cohesive team is the force that propels colleagues towards the summit of success, hand in hand."

*

A united team supports one another, overcoming obstacles and celebrating achievements together.

"The journey of collaboration embarks on a road of mutual trust, where every step leads to shared accomplishments."

*

Trust is the foundation of effective collaboration, ensuring colleagues can rely on one another to achieve their goals.

"The symphony of collaboration resonates in the hearts of colleagues, creating a melody of unity that echoes through the workplace."

*

A collaborative team creates a harmonious and united environment, where the spirit of cooperation reverberates throughout the organization.

"Through collaboration, we write the story of our shared success, chapter by chapter, with each colleague as a protagonist."

*

Colleagues co-author their journey to success, with each person playing a significant role in the team's achievements.

"When colleagues lift each other up, they soar to heights that were once beyond their reach."

*

A supportive team creates an uplifting environment, propelling each member to achieve their full potential.

"The tapestry of a successful team is woven with the threads of shared values and a shared vision."

*

A united team is aligned with a common set of values and a clear vision, which guide their actions and decisions.

"Like gears in a clock, each colleague's contribution is vital to keep the mechanism of the team functioning smoothly."

*

Just as gears work together to maintain the precision of a clock, colleagues' contributions are interconnected to keep the team running efficiently.

"The bonds of friendship formed through collaboration withstand the test of time, becoming the glue that holds a team together."

*

Collaborative relationships founded on trust and friendship create a strong bond that strengthens the team's cohesiveness.

"In the garden of teamwork, empathy waters the seeds of understanding, blossoming into a vibrant tapestry of unity."

*

Empathy cultivates a deep understanding of colleagues' perspectives, fostering a sense of unity and cooperation within the team.

"The power of synergy lies in the realization that together, we achieve more than the sum of our individual efforts."

*

Synergy occurs when colleagues combine their strengths and skills, resulting in outcomes that surpass what any individual could achieve alone.

"Colleagues who collaborate with humility are the architects of an inspiring workplace culture."

*

Humility fosters a collaborative environment, where colleagues are open to learning from one another and working together effectively.

- "The only place success comes before work is in the dictionary." - Vidal Sassoon

*

There are no shortcuts to success; hard work is the foundation of achieving your goals.

Conclusion

In conclusion, we spend approximately a fifth of our life in work therefore, it is important to make to most of this time and be happy in our chosen careers. Each of these quotes emphasizes differing aspects of our work life, inspiring us to embark on a journey of self-discovery, personal development and mindfulness.

Although the majority of the quotes are original and I have included a small selection of curated quotes from notable personalities and bastions of society know for their wisdom.

I hope you've enjoyed the read and have taken something positive from the words and sentiments.

There will be more books to follow.

"We're in this together"

For more information subscribe and follow me on:

Facebook

Twitter

TikTok

Instagram

Threads

WWW.Dragonish.rf.gd

Printed in Dunstable, United Kingdom

69153136R00131